animals**animals**

Moose

by **Diana Estigarribia**

Marshall Cavendish
Benchmark
New York

Series consultant
James G. Doherty
General Curator, Bronx Zoo, New York

Marshall Cavendish Benchmark
99 White Plains Road
Tarrytown, NY 10591-9001
www.marshallcavendish.us

Library of Congress Cataloging-in-Publication Data

Estigarribia, Diana.
Moose / by Diana Estigarribia.— 1st ed.
p. cm. — (Animals, animals)
Summary: "Describes the physical characteristics, behavior, and habitat of moose"—Provided by publisher.
Includes bibliographical references and index.
ISBN 0-7614-1870-9
1. Moose—Juvenile literature. I. Title. II. Series.

QL737.U55E78 2005
599.65'7—dc22
2004021444

Photo research by Joan Meisel

Cover photo: Patrick Frischnecht/Peter Arnold, Inc.
The photographs in this book are used by permission and through the courtesy of: *Animals Animals*: McDonald Wildlife
Photography, 1, 24; Louis Gagnon, 9; Marie Read, 17; James J. Stachecki, 26; Charles Palek, 27; Michael S. Bisceglie, 30;
Bill Silliker Jr., 36; Gary Griffen, 40. *Corbis*: Ron Sanford, 14; Alissa Crandell, 19; D. Robert Franz, 32; Robert Gehman, 34;
Lester V. Bergman, 35; Richard T. Nowitz, 38, 41. *Peter Arnold, Inc.*: Steve Kaufman, 4; S. J. Krasemann, 10, 11; Lior Rubin,
22; Patrick Frischknecht, 23, 42; Klaus Jost, 28. *Photo Researchers, Inc.*: Tom & Pat Leeson, 12.

Series design by Adam Mietlowski

Printed in China

1 3 5 6 4 2

Contents

1 Moose Matters

It is morning in the northern forest, and a moose is searching for food. It stops by a thick clump of brush and dips its large head in to eat. Suddenly there is a sharp noise close by. The moose stops eating and lifts its head. The moose may have poor eyesight, but its large ears pick up a range of sounds. No new noises follow, so after a few seconds, the moose goes back to its morning meal.

The moose is the largest member of the deer family, a group that also includes caribou, elk, and white-tailed deer. But unlike the other deer *species*, moose are usually *solitary* animals, preferring to live alone. In North America, moose are found in Canada,

Moose graze on a variety of trees and shrubs in the spring and summer.

CANADA

UNITED STATES

MOOSE

Alaska, and parts of the central United States, including Minnesota, North Dakota, Idaho, Montana, and Utah. Moose are also found in the northeastern United States, mostly in Vermont, New Hampshire, New York, Maine, and Connecticut, but in fewer numbers. A moose makes its home in and near the forests, swamps, and bodies of water found in these regions.

Relatives of the moose first arrived in North America tens of thousands of years ago. During the Ice Age, when parts of the earth were covered with sheets of ice, these mammals crossed the land bridge that existed at the time and connected Siberia (in eastern Asia) and North America.

Later, the moose, as we know it today, became an important part of the way of life and culture of North America's native peoples. The moose became part of the legends and the stories told by Native Americans. They also depended on the moose for their survival. They not only hunted it for its meat, they used moose skin and hair for clothing, blankets, and decoration. Even the bones were used to make tools. When the first European settlers arrived in North America, they also turned to the moose as a food source.

So many moose were hunted by Native Americans and settlers that the moose population began to shrink. Today moose are still hunted for their meat and as trophies, but laws limit the number that can be taken. In Europe, Canada, and the United States, hunters must have a permit or special license to hunt moose.

Species Chart

Adults
Length: 8 to 9 feet (2.4 to 2.7 meters)
Height: from the shoulder, about 6 feet (1.8 meters)
Weight: 600 to 1,800 pounds (272 to 817 kilograms)
Dewlap: up to 1 foot (30 centimeters)
Life Span: up to 15 years

Calves
Weight: at birth, 24 to 35 pounds (11 to 16 kilograms)

Antlers
Weight: 44 to 70 pounds (20 to 31.5 kilograms)
Width: between the antlers, up to 6 feet (1.8 meters)

Moose hooves are sharp and heavy, allowing the moose to move through thick layers of snow and to wade in ponds and marshes.

Moose have huge bodies. Measured from the hump on the shoulder, they can be more than 6 feet (1.8 meters) tall. A moose can weigh from 600 to 1,800 pounds (272 to 817 kilograms). Despite its huge size and weight, the moose is very *agile*. The moose's legs are long and thin like a horse's. Each of its feet is split into two large hoofed toes and two smaller toes. The moose can spread its toes to balance and steady itself. The *hooves* also help the moose to run fast. It can reach speeds up to 35 miles (56 kilometers) per hour.

The two smaller toes on the bottom of each hoof offer balance to the moose's long thin legs.

In Europe and Asia, moose are called elk.

The moose's head ends in a long, droopy n[...]
a wide top lip. Underneath the moose's chin is a [...]
skin called a *dewlap*. Male moose have larger [...]
than females. In some moose, the dewlap ca[...]
much as a foot (30 centimeters) long.

The moose's size helps it to survive ha[...]
winters. The moose's thick, furry coat is dar[...]
or black. The coat's long hair is hollow. It k[...]
moose warmer during the winter by helping to hold
in the moose's body heat. These hollow hairs also
float and help the moose glide across the water
when it goes for a swim.

Moose are mostly active during the day.
From dawn to dusk, they spend most of their
time searching for food.

Did You Know . . .

Isle Royale, an isolated island and national park in Lake Superior, has been home to moose since 1900. In 1948 the gray wolf was introduced to the island. Scientists have studied the two groups since 1959. They keep population counts and observe the animals' habits and how the two species interact and share the limited space of the island.

2 Growing a Set of Antlers

As the sun is about to rise, a young bull, or male, moose stirs from sleep. He moves silently through the forest, sniffing and picking at the trees and brush and looking for the leafiest spot.

The moose gets its name from a Native American word that means "twig eater." The moose is an *herbivore*, an animal that eats only plants. It survives on a mixture of leaves, twigs, bark, and shrubs. Its favorite foods are the leaves of aspen, birch, and willow trees. Thirty-two powerful teeth help the moose to bite down and scrape off the tough bark from trees. The moose is so tall that it can reach many high tree branches. A moose will even stand up on its hind legs

Moose use their strong teeth to strip leaves off branches.

to get to branches as high as 10 feet (3 meters). When it eats, it moves its mouth along the branch, the way people eat an ear of corn. A moose can eat for hours without stopping and can take in as much as 44 pounds (20 kilograms) of food each day.

The moose is a kind of animal called a *ruminant*. A ruminant's stomach has four parts. These sections help the moose to digest food. Leaves and plant matter are stored in one section and, after a short time, the food returns to the mouth where the moose continues to chew it. This is called "chewing cud."

In the summer, flies and other insects buzz around the moose's head. To find relief and to escape the insects, the moose often heads to a nearby lake or pond. The moose walks into the water until it is almost completely covered.

Wading in ponds and lakes offers the moose more than just comfort. Moose also find food at the bottom. A moose can plunge 20 feet (6 meters) and hold its breath underwater for more than a minute while it searches for plants to eat. Moose need underwater plants in their diet. They provide the moose with salt and other minerals. In the winter, when lakes and

Moose live near lakes and ponds, where they can stay cool in the summer.

ponds are frozen over and the leaves have fallen off the trees, moose dig through the snow to find berries, branches, and grass. A moose gains most of its weight in the summer. This is also the time of year when a bull grows its *antlers*.

Deer are the only animals that grow antlers. Among moose, only the males sport these bony growths on top of their heads. When a bull is one year old, its first set of antlers begins growing. The first set of antlers is usually short and spiky. The bull's forehead develops two bumps called *pedicles*. A pedicle is shaped like a small, round knob. A layer of thin, furry hair called *velvet* covers the growing antlers and helps them to become large and powerful.

Every year, around September or October, the velvet begins to fall off the antler. The bull shakes its head or rubs its antlers against the trunks of large trees until all the velvet has been removed. What remains is the moose's smooth, bony antlers. The antlers look like large hands with the fingers spread out. The antlers grow very fast, taking less than six months to reach their full size. Antlers can weigh from 44 to 70 pounds (20 to 31.5 kilograms) and can be as wide as 6 feet (1.8 meters). One of the largest set of antlers was found in Alaska. It was 6.5 feet (2 meters) wide.

The velvet on a bull's antlers begins to peel off when the moose is ready to mate.

The Moose:

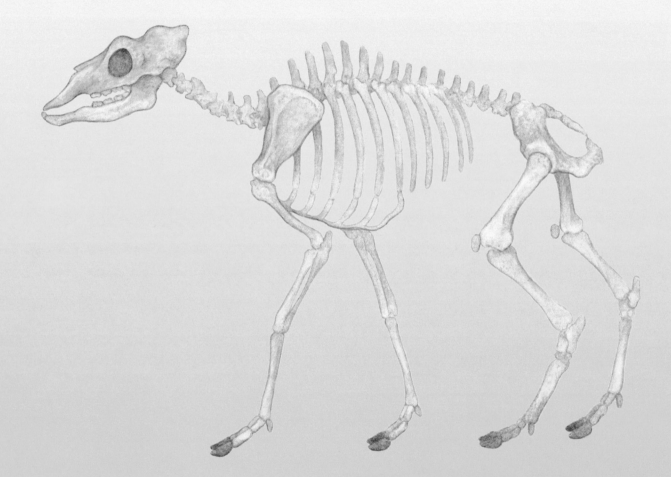

A moose's long legs allow it to run fast and escape danger.

Inside and Out

They also help the moose to feed on tree branches that are hard to reach.

The moose keeps its antlers for only a few months. Then in winter, it sheds them. This is called *casting*. The antlers are left behind on the forest floor where other small animals, such as mice, eat them. They are drawn to the minerals and other *nutrients* the antlers contain.

The next spring, the bull moose starts growing another set of antlers. Each new set of antlers gets bigger as a bull ages. A bull's antlers are biggest when it is between seven and ten years old.

In the winter, a bull's antlers fall off so new antlers can start growing the following spring.

Antlers are important during the *rut*, or mating season. Bulls compete for females, called cows. Sometimes a young bull fights an older, larger bull during the rut. The older bulls tend to be better and more experienced at fighting than younger moose. When the two bulls face off, they dip their heads and swing their antlers from side to side. The victor then gets to mate with the female. A cow is ready to mate when she is about two years old. For the cow, a whole new cycle of life begins with the mating season.

A fight during the rut is usually over quickly. Two bulls push and lock horns for a short time until one bull retreats.

3 A Mother and Her Calves

After the rut is over, a cow prepares to become a mother. By springtime, usually in May, after carrying the calf for eight months, a cow is ready to give birth. Moose can give birth to twins or sometimes triplets, but usually only one calf is born each year. A newborn calf can weigh from 24 to 35 pounds (11 to 16 kilograms).

After giving birth, a cow keeps her offspring near a reliable food source. A cow must eat more than 60 pounds (27 kilograms) of food every day so she can produce enough milk for her calf. A calf grows quickly, gaining more than 2 pounds (1 kilogram) each day during its first five months of life.

A cow and her calf live together for a year.

The newborn's fur is a light reddish brown. Over the next couple of months, the calf's coat becomes darker.

The cow stays close to her calf at all times. Although adult moose live alone, mothers and calves live together for about a year. It is an important time in a calf's life, when a mother teaches her young the skills it will need as an adult.

One of the first things a mother teaches her calf is how to swim. The cow brings her calf to the lake or pond often, nudging and coaxing it deeper into the water until it is no longer afraid.

Moose are strong swimmers and learn to swim at an early age.

Moose calves lack the skills to protect themselves against predators.

After a few days of teaching, the calf and the mother can swim together with ease. Moose usually start swimming a few weeks after they are born.

A mother cow's most important job is to care for her young. The calf is most *vulnerable* during its first month of life. The mother carefully guards the calf against *predators* such as wolves or bears. When a predator threatens a calf, the mother fights to protect her young.

27

Bears hunt moose especially during the spring, when newborn calves are most vulnerable.

She uses her powerful hooves and back legs to kick at the wolf or bear. Then the moose use their speedy legs to try and escape the attacker.

Bears come out of *hibernation* during the spring, the same time that calves are born. Where both animals share a habitat, bears may eat as many as half of the calves born each year. But the greatest threat the moose faces is the wolf. Wolves hunt and kill both newborn and adult moose.

Did You Know . . .

Moose are quiet animals, except when they have something important to say. Bulls and cows grunt to attract each other during the rut. Calls can be heard as far as one-third of a mile (0.5 kilometer) away. A cow also communicates with her calf by grunting. The cow grunts to her calf when she wants it to stay still, to follow along, or when it is time to eat.

4 A Dangerous Life

Life in the woods presents plenty of dangers. Young calves are killed by hungry predators. Old or sick moose that are too weak to defend themselves are also easy targets. Even young, healthy moose must be careful. While moose have poor eyesight, a healthy moose can smell a potential threat from far away. A moose's hearing is also very sharp. It can listen closely for the movement and approach of a predator.

Moose are so large that few animals want to attack them. Only the grizzly bear is larger and stronger than the moose. A grizzly uses its claws and large paws to overpower a moose. A moose is not strong enough to beat a grizzly bear in a fight.

Moose use their strong sense of smell and hearing to detect predators.

Moose often fall prey to gray wolves in the winter, when the moose cannot move as quickly in the heavy snow.

Winter is a dangerous time for moose, when the cold and snow make it harder to survive. Finding enough food is hard work. Plants have died and dried up, and all the leaves are gone from the trees. Moose lose weight during the winter and can become weak and sick. That makes them easy prey for wolves. To make matters worse, a moose cannot move quickly through the deep snow. When a moose gets stuck in the snow, wolves can surround the moose and attack it.

But the moose has a way to defend itself. Winter is the only time that adult moose come together to form groups. As many as a dozen moose will follow each other single file through the deep snow. This is called *yarding*. Their dark coats stand out against the white snow piled several feet high. Two or more adult moose trample the snow, pacing back and forth to tamp it down. After a few minutes, they create a path in the snow for the other moose to use. With the snow packed and tamped down, they can more easily dig and find buried grasses and plants. Together, they can *forage* while defending themselves against wolves at the same time. But the moose must be careful. They can easily become trapped in the deep snow tunnels they create.

In a process called yarding, moose trudge single file through the snow.

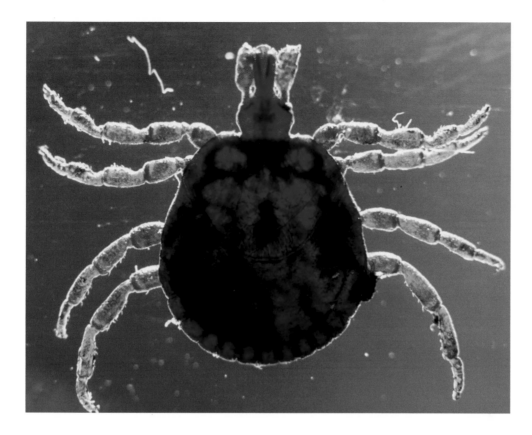

The cold season is when the moose fights another of its enemies, the winter tick. The winter tick is a tiny creature, like an insect, that targets only moose. Hundreds of ticks land on the moose and begin biting its skin. A single moose can be covered with as many as 100,000 ticks. Moose rub their bodies against trees or brush to try to get the ticks off. The ticks make some moose itch so much that they lick, chew, and rub their own fur until patches of their coat wear off.

During the winter months, moose can die from disease or lack of food.

These are called "ghost moose" because of their light gray coloring. The ticks can cause a moose to lose half its blood, leaving it very weak. A moose can die from a severe attack of ticks.

Natural predators are just one of the threats moose face. Moose can wander out of the forest into areas where people live. Or the opposite can happen. People move to the places where moose live, shrinking and changing the animal's habitat.

5 Moose and People

People build new communities near the wooded areas where moose live. Trees and large stretches of forest are often cut down. These actions can harm the moose and change its habitat. Groups of moose may not have enough food to support them all. The habitat can become too small to support the moose population it once did. Saving a moose's habitat is one of the most important ways people can protect this animal's future.

When a moose reaches the edge of a forest, it may wander out onto nearby roads. In the winter, it is easier for moose to follow paved roads where the snow has been removed. Moose also like to eat the salt used

Moose are curious animals that will approach humans and even places where people live.

39

to cover roads in winter. This increases the risk that they will be hit by cars. In Alaska, six hundred moose die every year in accidents with cars. Moose also sometimes walk along railroad tracks where they can be hit by trains.

Moose are drawn to the salt used on winter roads.

In modern times, moose have lived in closer and closer contact with people. When Europeans first settled North America, there were tens of thousands of moose living on the continent. In the 1800s, there were no laws protecting wildlife like the moose.

Moose can live for up to fifteen years in the wild.

Hunters could kill as many moose as they wanted. By the early 1900s, because of too much hunting, moose had disappeared from many states.

Today, moose are protected by laws in North America and Europe. In the United States, those states with moose populations allow only a small number of bulls to be hunted each year. Hunting calves is not permitted. These rules keep hunters from killing too many moose.

But some people hunt moose illegally. This is called *poaching*. The government of Ontario, Canada, started a program called Moose Watch to protect moose from illegal hunting.

Other people like to go to northern forests to see the moose in its natural habitat. Seeing an adult bull or a mother and calves in the wild is a rare treat. With wise controls and the help of people, moose will continue to have long and healthy lives in the forests of the world.

Did You Know . . .

Did you know that moose like to eat Christmas trees? On the Canadian islands of Newfoundland and Labrador, moose graze on the native balsam, a type of evergreen tree. To prevent moose from eating too many of the balsam, some growers have moved their tree farms to areas where there are fewer moose.

Glossary

agile: Able to move quickly.

antlers: Horns that grow from a bull moose's head.

casting: When a bull moose's antlers fall off.

dewlap: The bell-shaped piece of skin that hangs from a moose's throat.

forage: To wander in search of food.

habitat: The place where a plant or animal lives.

herbivore: An animal that eats only plants.

hibernation: A period, usually in winter, when an animal is not active.

hoof: The hard, protective covering of an animal's toes.

nutrients: The minerals found in food.

pedicle: One of the two bony bumps on a male moose's forehead that grows into an antler.

poaching: Hunting animals in places or at certain times when it is not allowed.

predator: An animal that preys on, or eats, other animals to survive.

ruminant: A type of animal that chews its cud and usually has a four-part stomach.

rut: The time of year when moose mate.

solitary: Living or being alone.

species: An animal that shares the same characteristics and mates only with its own kind.

velvet: The fuzzy skin that forms around a bull moose's antlers.

vulnerable: At risk or in danger.

yarding: When a group of moose pack down snow by walking on it.

Find Out More

Books

DuTemple, Lesley A. *North American Moose*. Minneapolis, MN: Carolrhoda Books, 2001.

Fair, Jeff. *Moose for Kids: (Moose Are Like That)*. Minacqua, WI: NorthWord Press, 1992.

Geist, Valerius. *Moose: Behavior, Ecology, Conservation*. Stillwater, MN: Voyageur Press, 1999.

Taylor, Bonnie Highsmith. *Roscoe: A North American Moose*. Logan, IA: Perfection Learning, 2000.

Rodgers, Art. *Moose*. Stillwater, MN: Voyageur Press, 2001.

Silliker, Bill. *Moose: Giants of the Northern Forest*. Richmond Hill, Ontario: Firefly Books, 1998.

Web Sites

Animal Planet Mammal Guide: Moose
http://animal.discovery.com/guides/mammals/habitat/northforest/moose.html

National Park Service—Isle Royale
http://www.nps.gov/isro/index.htm

The Wolves and Moose of Isle Royale
http://www.isleroyalewolf.org/

Yellowstone National Park—Moose
http://www.nps.gov/yell/nature/animals/moose/moose.html

Index

Page numbers for illustrations are in **boldface**.

About the Author

Diana Estigarribia is the author of *Smithsonian National Zoological Park* from the Great Zoos of the United States series. She has also written books on the life sciences, plants, and animal habitats. She is a journalist and researcher for a national magazine and lives in New York with her husband, a novelist and book designer.